WHAT IS AN OPEN AIR MUSEUM?

You have probably visited an ordinary museum before, most likely a large building full of glass cases containing interesting things like old coins, pots, and weapons, but in an open air museum the exhibits are generally so big they would never fit into glass cases!

This is because this Museum is a museum of old houses, farm buildings and other buildings such as craftsmen's workshops.

They are houses and buildings that were once going to be destroyed. In so many villages and towns today lovely old buildings are being pulled down so that brand new buildings can be put up instead. Sometimes roads are widened and then lots of houses have to be knocked down.

It is to save some of these fine old historic buildings from being smashed by the bulldozer that they are carefully taken to pieces and brought to the Museum for safety and for you to see.

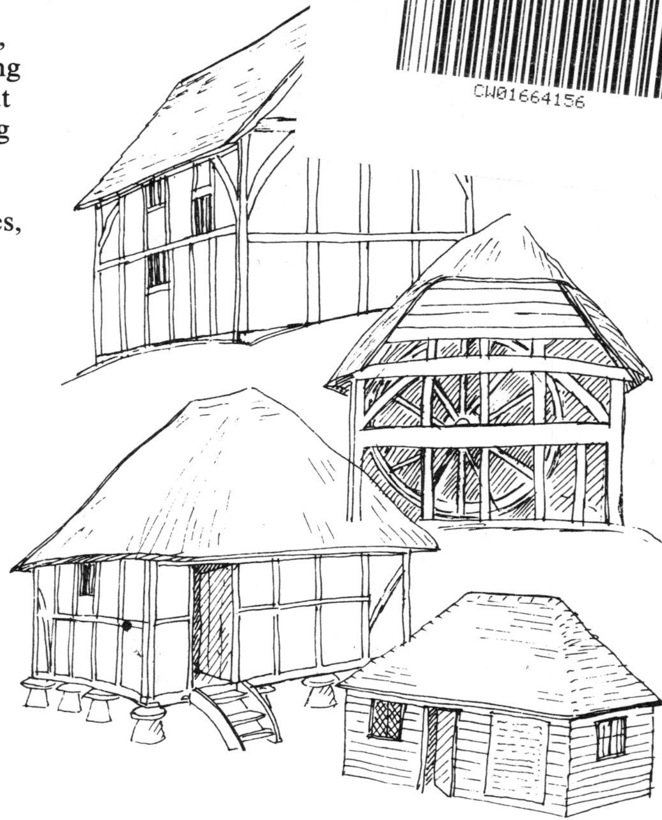

THE BARN

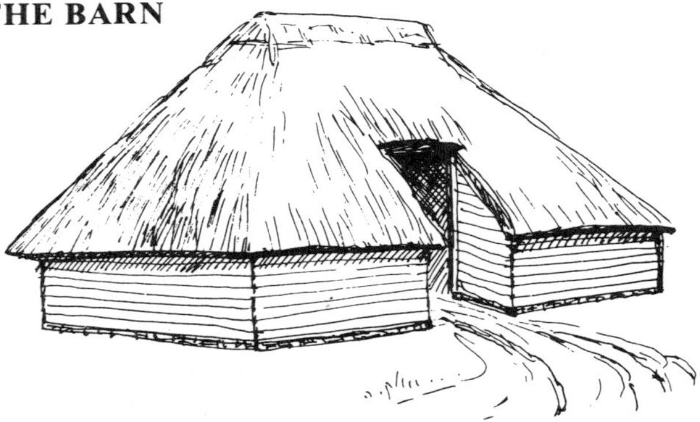

The thatched barn came from Priors Leaze Farm at Hambrook, a few miles west of Chichester. High up on one of the roof rafters and out of sight is the tiny inscription shown on the right. This is almost certainly the date when the barn was built, and the initials probably those of the craftsman who did the original building work. Inside the barn you will see a timber-frame, around which is a continuous aisle on all four sides. This is a type of layout once fairly common in the western part of Sussex and the eastern part of Hampshire, but now rather rare as many have been pulled down.

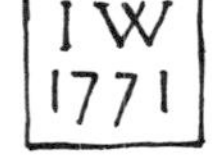

The barn was often the biggest of all the buildings on a farm, and was used for storing and threshing cereal crops such as wheat, barley, and oats. When all the harvest had been gathered into the barn the threshing took place. Threshing separates the grain from the stalk, and provided winter work for the farm worker. To do the threshing the crop was beaten with a special tool called a flail.

The picture on the right shows two flails in use. They were each made of two pieces of wood. At the end of the handle part was a knot of raw hide (often the underside of a horse's tail), to which was joined a very tough piece of wood called a swingle. The swingle did the beating. Do you know what has replaced the flail in modern farming?

Inside the barn there is an exhibition about the work of the Museum.

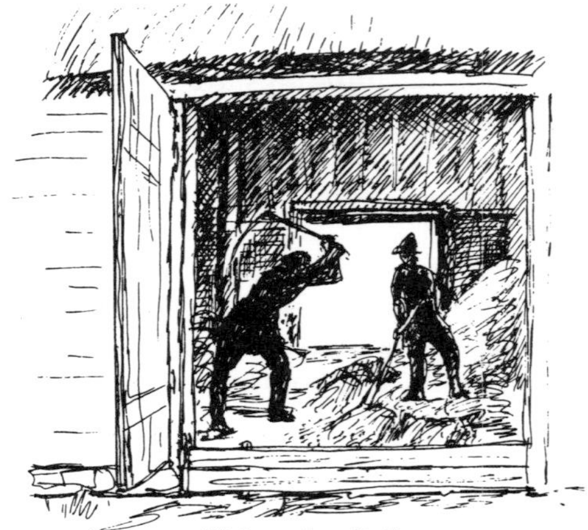

Using the flail

THE TREAD WHEEL

Here is a piece of machinery nearly 400 years old and still working!

The great wooden wheel, which came from a little village in Hampshire called Catherington, was used for bringing up water from a very deep well. A man, or a donkey, turned the huge axle and wound up the bucket by walking inside the wheel. You could walk miles and go nowhere!

There is not a proper well here with water underneath the wheel, but a hole has been dug and lined with bricks like a proper well so that the bucket can go into the ground to show visitors how it once worked.

Look carefully at the little house it is in. Look at the walls and see how they are made. This is exactly the way in which people hundreds of years ago made their walls. It is thought that the wheel and the little house were built about the year 1600, in other words made in the time of Elizabethan England.

You can see another wheel like this at Carisbrooke Castle on the Isle of Wight.

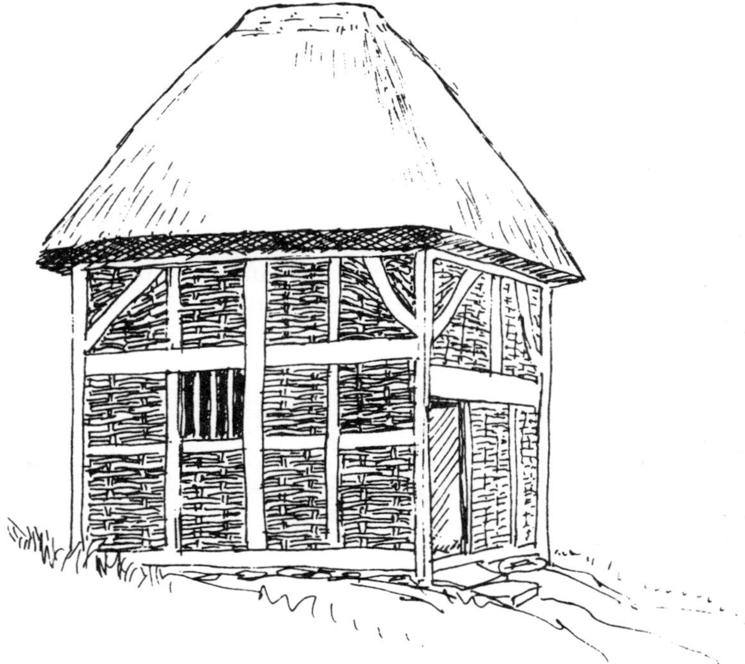

WINKHURST

This is a farmhouse built about 1400, the sort of house a farmer lived in nearly a hundred years before Christopher Columbus sailed to America.

It was given to the Museum because the valley in which is stood (near Edenbridge in Kent) has been flooded to make a reservoir.

Before you step inside, walk right round the house. How many windows can you find? Not many, so not much light would have got inside. Notice there's no glass, just wooden bars.

Now look at the great timbers that make the framework of the house. Some are so old they are black with age. The lighter coloured wood is of course new and was put in because the older timber was too rotten to use.

Notice how the timbers are fastened together. Not with nails and screws, but with long wooden pegs driven in with a hammer. These wooden pegs hold the buildings together, and so are very important.

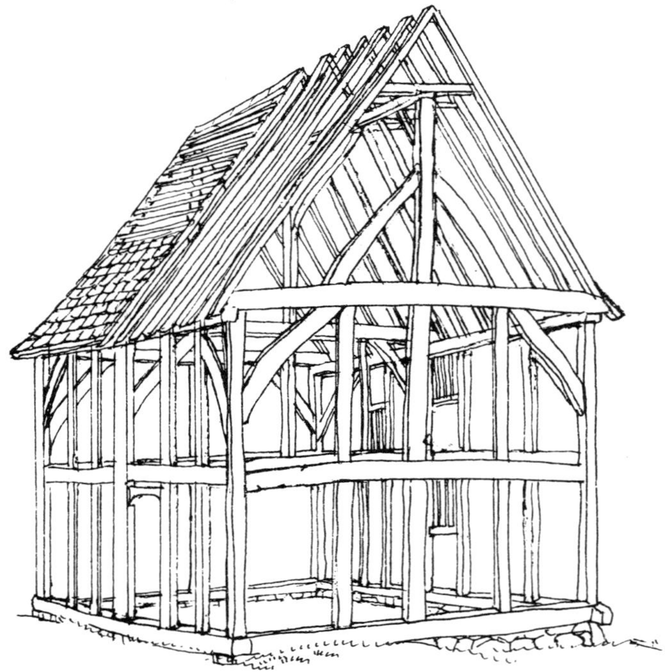

Inside the house you can see the living quarters on the ground floor. The furniture is not old, although all pieces are copies of the type of furniture the medieval farmer would have used. Near one end, in the middle of the floor, is the fire. We can imagine all the family merrily chatting as they sat around a crackling log fire after a hard day's work in the fields, or talking about the Battle of Agincourt, which took place about the time when Winkhurst was built. It must have been very cosy in such a little house.

Look up and see where the smoke went out. Not through a chimney like you have at home, but through a hole in the shape of a triangle. Up there the old rafters are covered in soot from the smoke of hundreds of years ago.

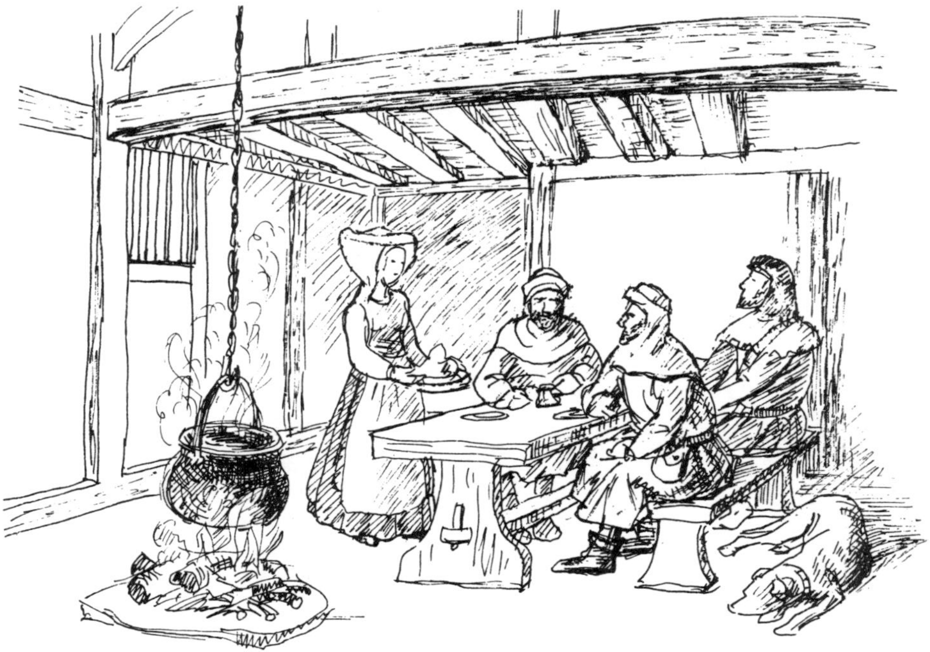

Climb the stairs and you'll be in the sleeping quarter. This part is called the solar. Look closely at the wall where it has been left unplastered so that you can see how it has been made. It is made of strips of wood, woven together. This is called a wattle wall.

The outside walls are made of wattle as well, but these walls are covered with plaster to keep out the rain and wind. The plaster is called daub, and so the outside walls are called wattle and daub walls.

THE SAW PIT

Before saw mills were first used all the timber for building had to be cut by hand. When the trees had been felled and cut into shorter lengths, the logs were taken to saw pits like this and were rolled over the top of the pit.

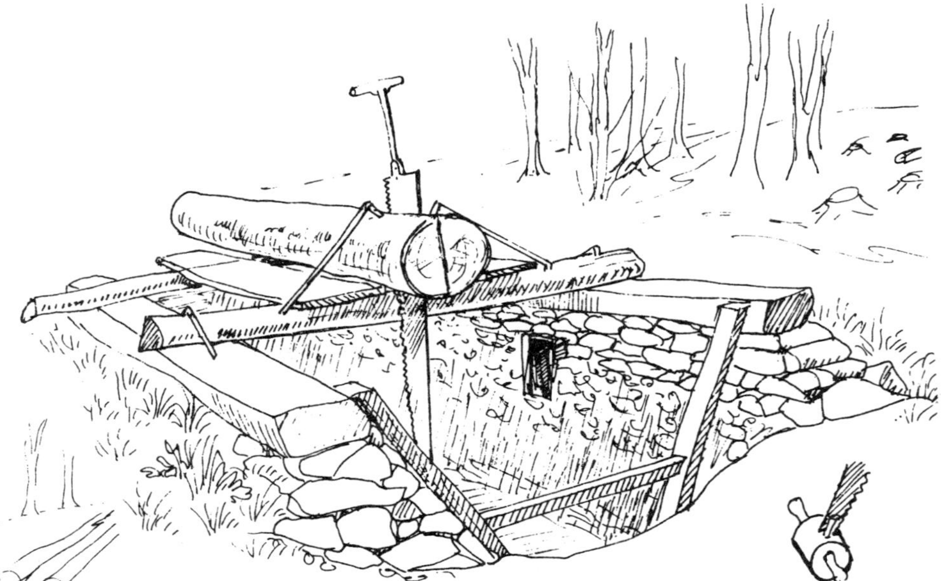

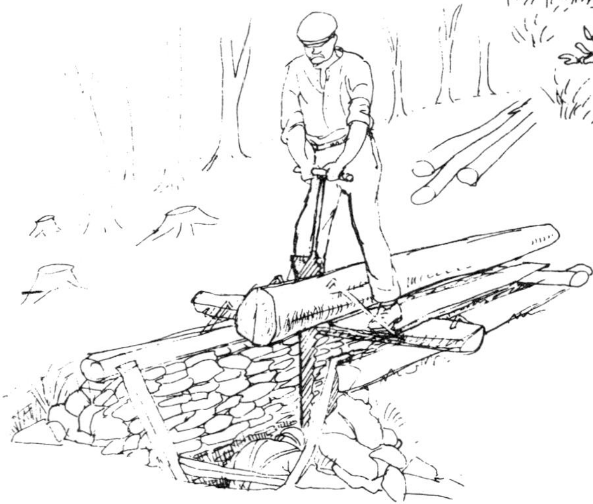

Two men (called sawyers) sawed up the wood. One man (the bottom sawyer) stood in the pit (and got covered with saw-dust!) while the other man (the top sawyer) stood on top and guided the saw as it cut. The long saw they used is called a pit saw.

TIME CHART

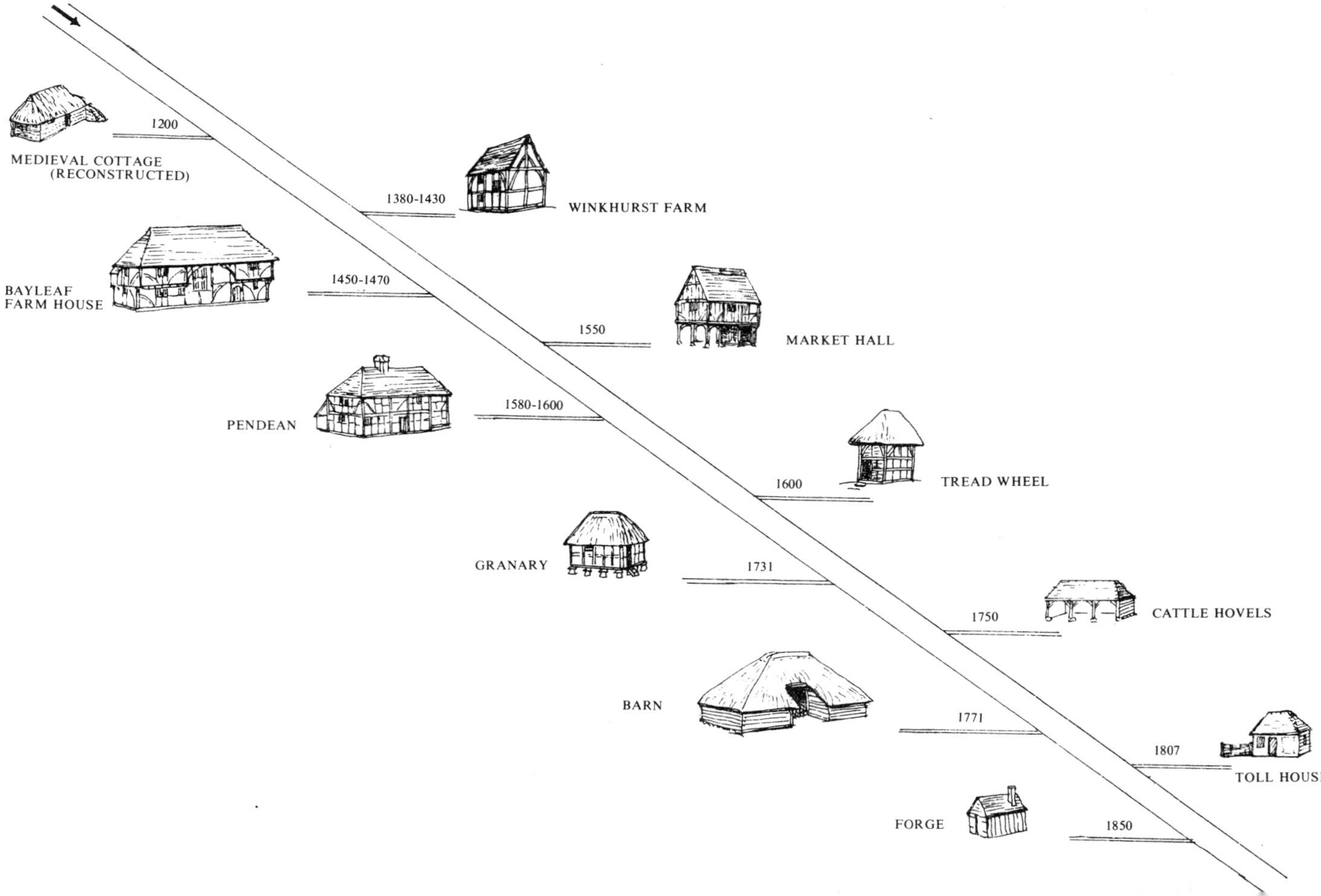

1200
MEDIEVAL COTTAGE (RECONSTRUCTED)
1380-1430
WINKHURST FARM
1450-1470
BAYLEAF FARM HOUSE
1550
MARKET HALL
1580-1600
PENDEAN
1600
TREAD WHEEL
1731
GRANARY
1750
CATTLE HOVELS
1771
BARN
1807
TOLL HOUSE
1850
FORGE

THE CHARCOAL BURNER'S CAMP

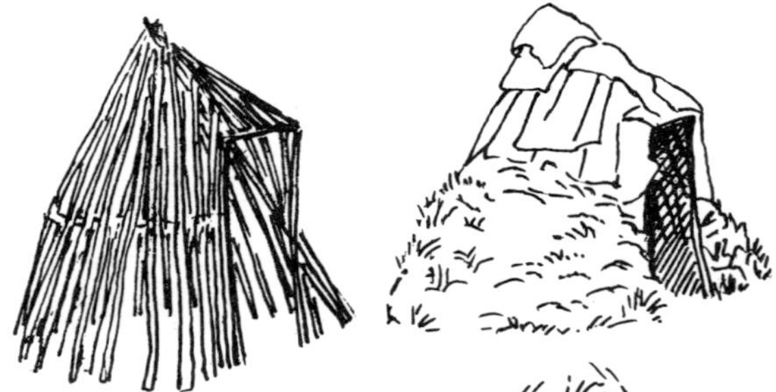

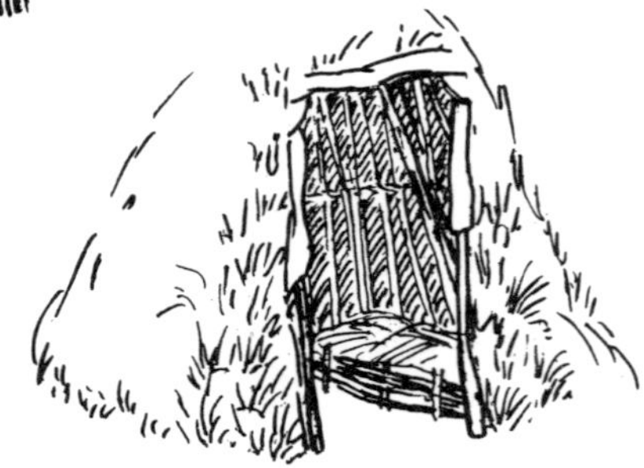

Charcoal is partly burnt wood, and years ago was very important in Sussex, Surrey and Kent because it was used in iron making and for making gunpowder.
Charcoal was used because it gives about twice the heat of wood. To make charcoal the wood must be burnt in a special way by an expert charcoal burner.

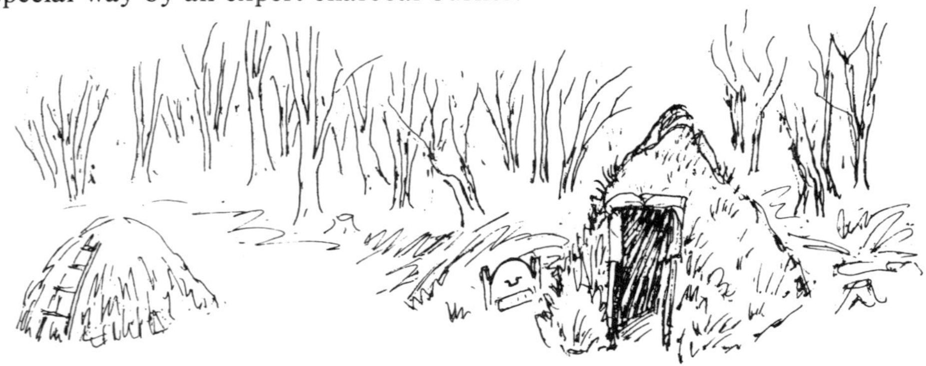

The charcoal burner lived in the woods near his work. He lived in a tiny hut made of long poles which were covered with sacking and then piled over with turf. Inside is a bed made of hazel twigs and covered with leaves. No soft mattress! Imagine sleeping on this bed after a hard day's work!

If the charcoal burner was living in the woods with his family then he would have made a larger turf-covered hut to serve as a living room. One of these is also shown in the camp.

The charcoal was made by building a pile of wood in a special way and then lighting it through a hole in the top centre. To show how the pile of wood, or kiln as it is called, was built up, four different stages in the construction are shown.

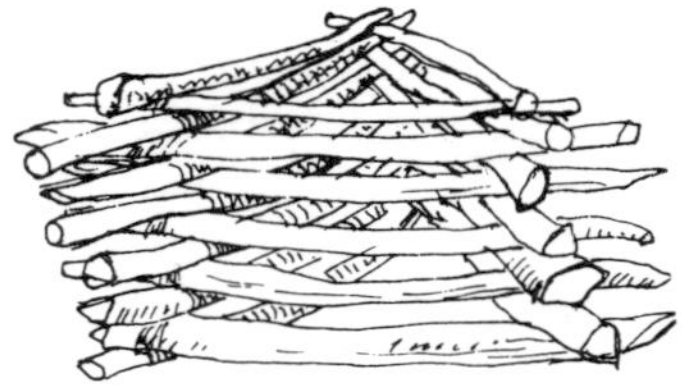

STAGE 1

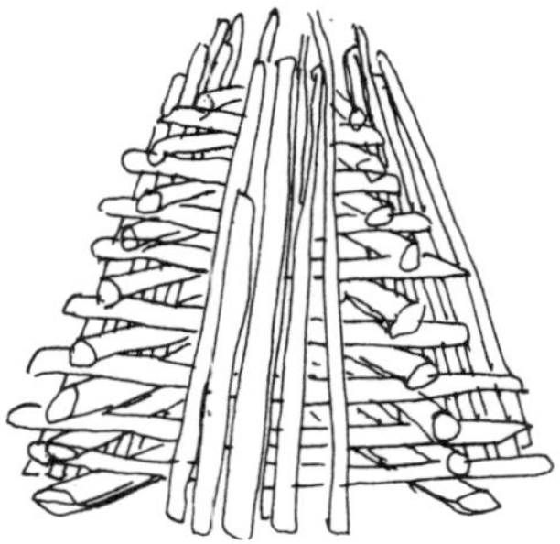

STAGE 2

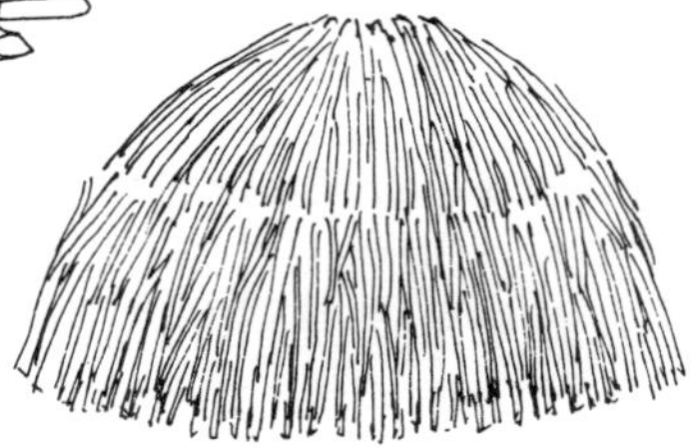

STAGE 3

When all the wood had been arranged it was covered with earth or pieces of turf — anything to stop the kiln bursting into flames when it had been lit. It must never burst into flames or it would burn too quickly and only ashes would be left! It used to take three days and two nights to burn the kiln and then it was put out by throwing water over it.

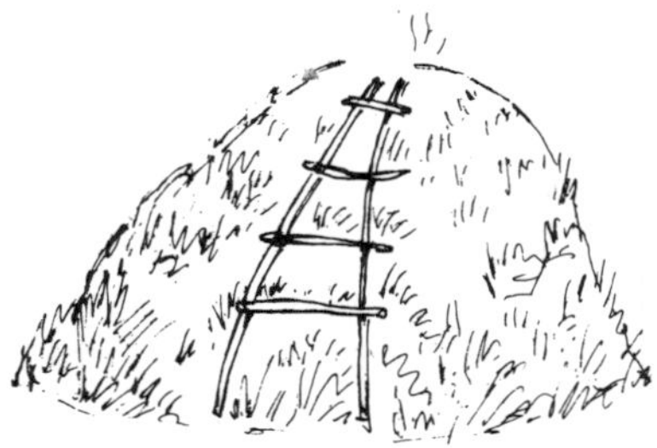

STAGE 4

Charcoal is still used today, but is made in a different way. Today it is used for making certain chemicals, for charcoal biscuits for dogs, and people still often use charcoal when they have barbecues. Do you know where charcoal can be bought today?

THE MEDIEVAL COTTAGE

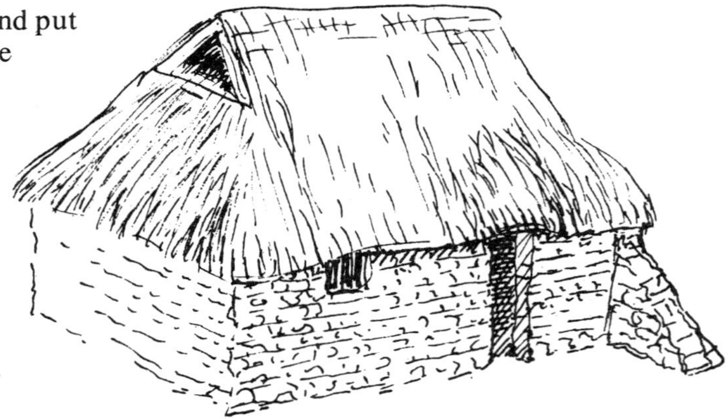

This is NOT an old building that has been taken down and put up again. Rather it is a copy of what a medieval cottage was probably like.

The walls of the cottage are built of flint, which is one of the strongest materials to be found on the chalk downs. The roof is covered with reed thatch. Note the very low doorway (4 feet 9 inches high), and the two very small windows. The small size of the openings made in these early buildings was probably because of the need to keep in as much warmth as possible, and to keep out any bad weather. This of course had the unfortunate result of keeping much light and fresh air from the inside.

Inside the cottage there is just one room. This is a living room and work room combined, for in the corner at one end there is a baking oven. In the middle of the floor is an open hearth for cooking and heating the cottage. Smoke could escape from the triangular openings at each end of the roof, a feature known as a gablet.

The original cottage from which this copy was built was excavated by archaeologists at Hangleton, in the north part of Hove, where it formed part of a small downland village, now lost and covered over with modern houses and two golf courses. From the evidence of pottery dug up, this particular cottage is thought to have been built about 1250. This would place its date in the reign of King Henry III.

PENDEAN

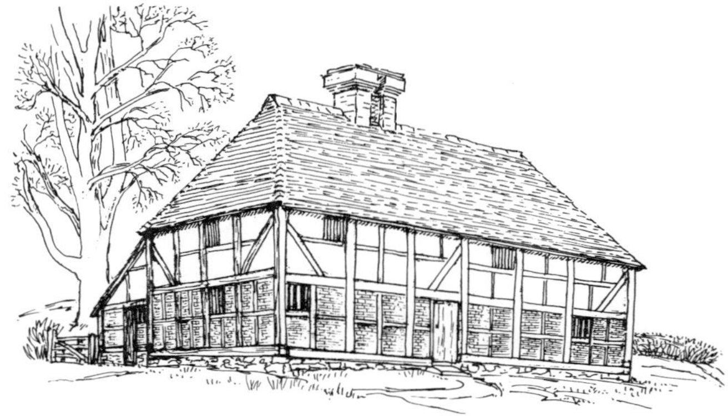

Pendean was built at the end of the Tudor period, sometime during the reign of Queen Elizabeth I. It originally stood at Pendean Farm at West Lavington, just south of Midhurst.

It was saved by the Museum when it was in danger of being destroyed to make way for the quarrying of sand. Today the Pendean Sandpit provides the building industry with thousands of tons of sand every year.

This lovely old farmhouse shows some of the ways in which builders of the Tudor period improved their houses as they tried to make them better than the medieval ones. If you compare Pendean with the medieval farmhouses of Winkhurst and Bayleaf at the Museum you will see how some of these improvements were being made.

One of the biggest differences is that Pendean has a large brick chimney so that all the smoke from the fire could be funnelled up out of the roof. In Winkhurst and Bayleaf the fireplace is right in the middle of the floor, and the smoke had to find its way out of the house as best it could. When the smoke did not escape quickly it must have been very uncomfortable, with lots of watery eyes! Home life must have been much more comfortable as the use of the chimney became more and more popular in the sixteenth century. Downstairs there are two large fireplaces. Built into the side of one of these fireplaces (the one in the left-hand side room as you come through the front door) there is a little oven.

Another thing the Tudors did to improve their houses was to make much more use of brick. Pendean has the walls of the ground floor built of brick, but notice that the upper walls were still made in the old fashioned medieval way, using wattle and daub.

BAYLEAF

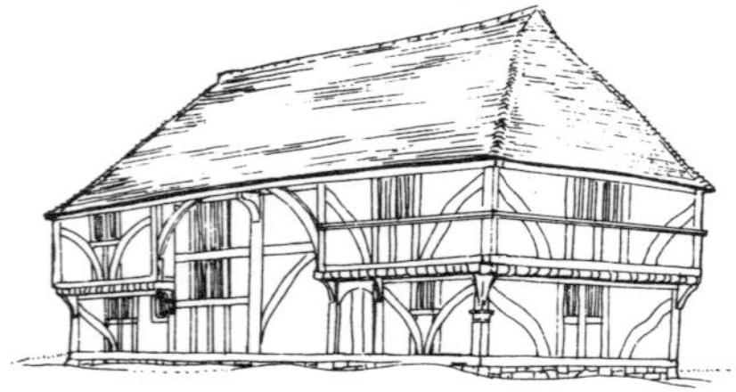

Bayleaf is a farmhouse built about 1450 for a prosperous farmer in Kent. Like Winkhurst it too came from near Edenbridge because it was in the same valley flooded to make a reservoir.
Notice features you have already seen at Winkhurst — the timber frame, use of wooden pegs, wattle and daub walls, windows with bars, and without glass. But Bayleaf shows all the signs of being a much finer building. Its size and fine craftsmanship suggest that Bayleaf was the home of a fairly well-to-do family.

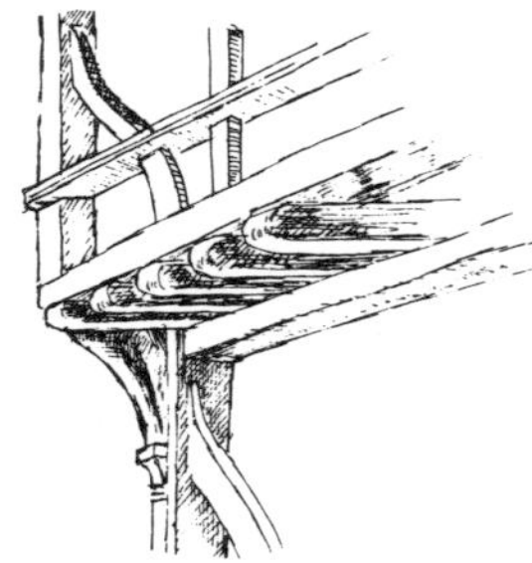

Before you go inside notice that part of the first floor is built out so that the floor overhangs the downstairs part. This is called jettying, and gives more floor space upstairs.

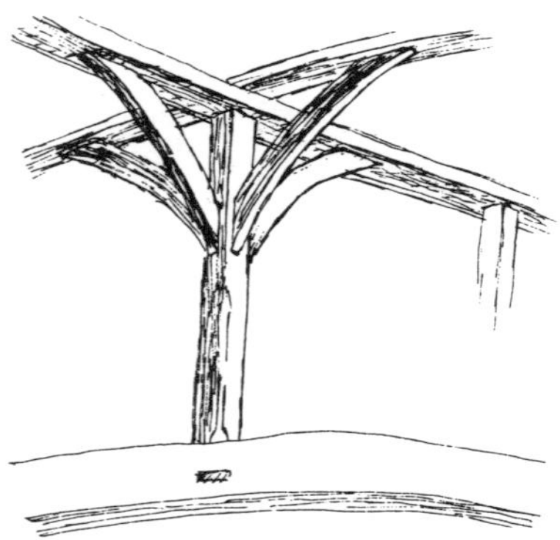

Go inside through the passage: on one side is the service end containing the pantry and buttery where food was stored and prepared. On the other side is the hall, or main living room, where family and friends would meet together for meals and entertainments. Look up and you will see the crown post — a vertical wooden post with outstretched arms that helps support the roof. From the hall is reached the private quarter of the house, with the bedroom area. This is the solar end. At the solar end, and jutting out from the first floor, is a reconstruction of a medieval lavatory, called a garderobe.

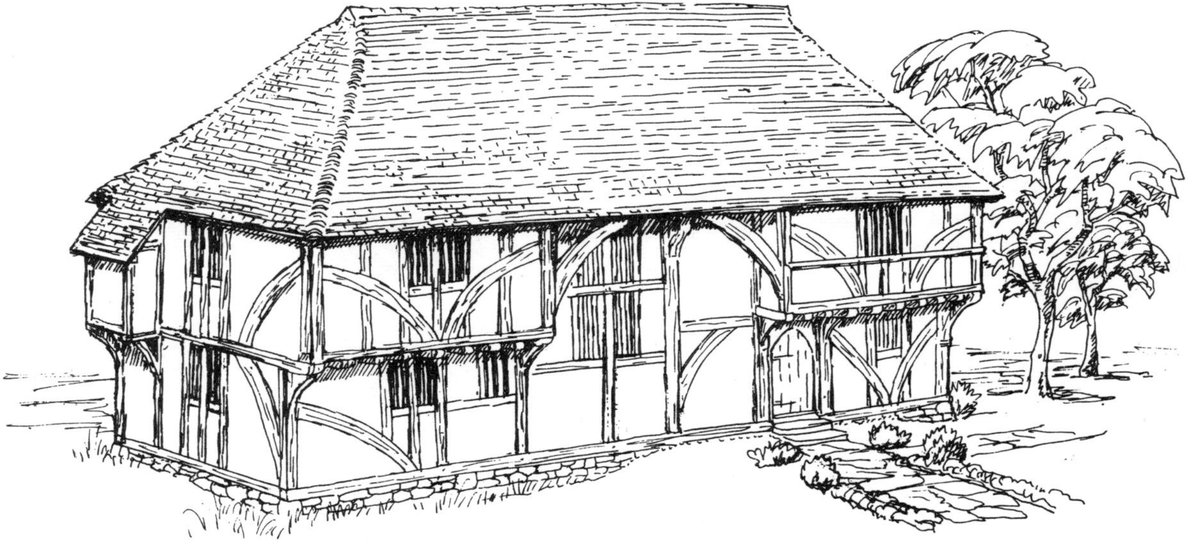

Bayleaf

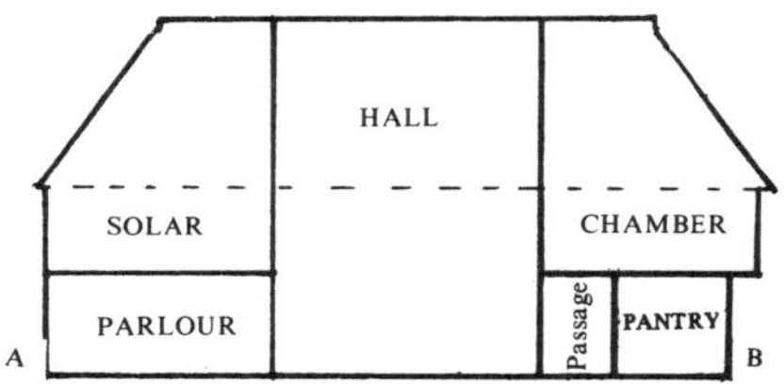

Elevation

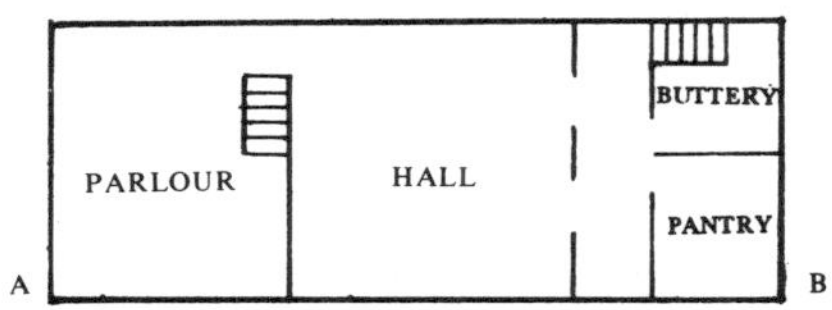

Plan — lower floor

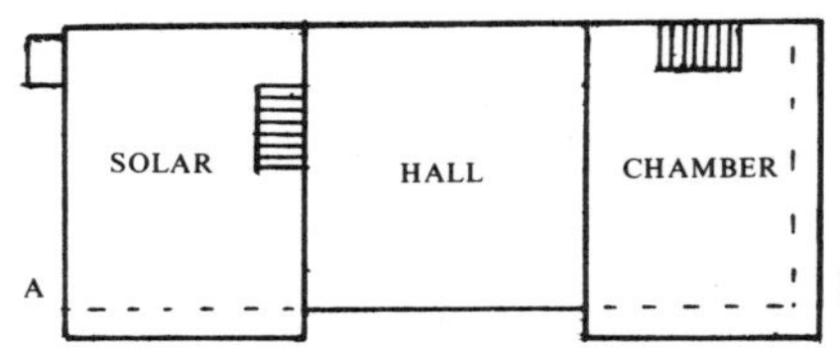

Plan — upper floor

THE CATTLE SHEDS

Near Bayleaf there are two cattle sheds. The one near the Granary comes from Lurgashall, near Petworth, the other, behind Bayleaf, from Kirdford, also near Petworth.

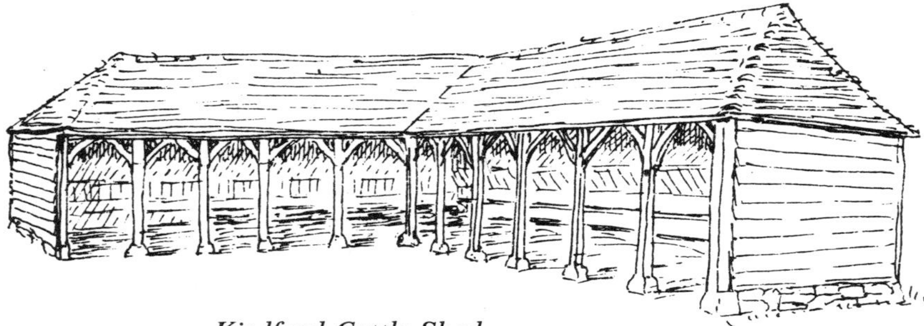

Kirdford Cattle Shed

Both cattle sheds were built originally about the mid-18th century, and were used for giving shelter when the weather was bad, and a place where cattle could be fed in the dry. An old name for a cattle shed is a hovel.

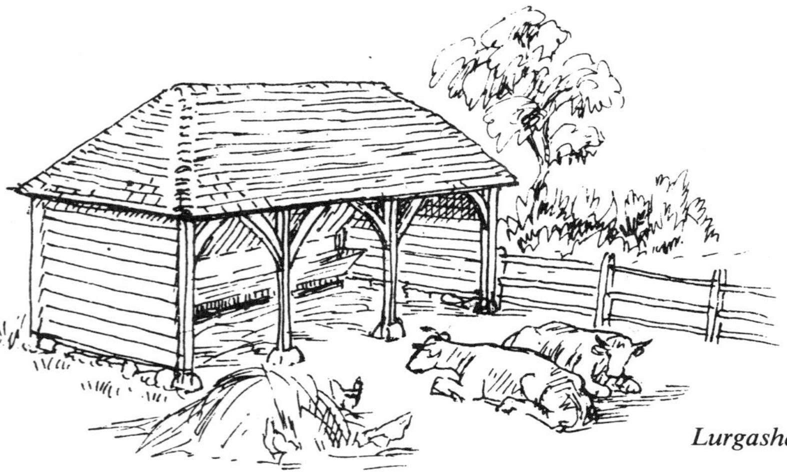

Lurgashall Cattle Shed

THE GRANARY

This is a special type of barn farmers built for storing grain. It is known as a granary, and came from Littlehampton. It was brought to the Museum for preservation as it was going to be pulled down because of the building of a new road.

Notice that it stands on 16 stones. They are called staddle stones and look something like mushrooms. Do you see why? The reason for having them was that damp from the ground could not reach the grain and turn it mouldy, and it also stopped mice and rats from getting inside.

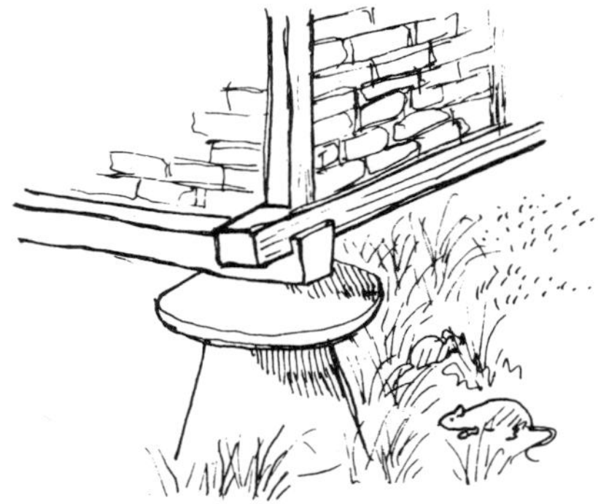

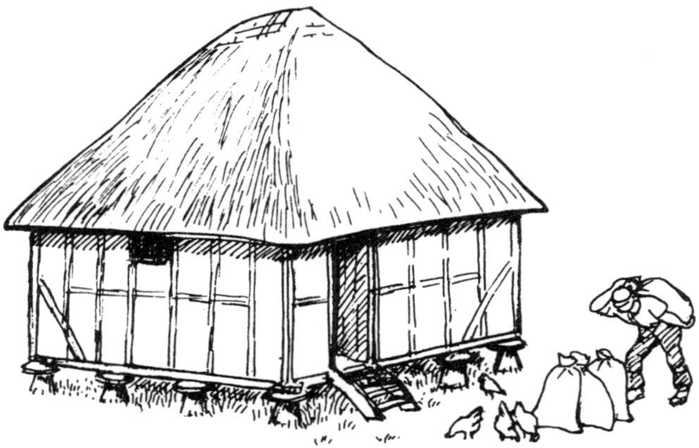

Before you go inside, have a look for a wooden grill in one of the walls. Can you think why this was made? Now go and find a brick which has a date cut into it. Why do you think a date was put there?

THE MARKET HALL

This timber-framed Market Hall came from Titchfield, near Fareham in Hampshire. It was probably built about 1550, during the time of the Tudor kings and queens. It has been brought to the Museum because it was falling to pieces and was very dangerous.

Market halls like this were once fairly common throughout England. The lower part, usually without side walls, was used as a market place where merchants could set up their stalls on market day. The weekly market was once far more important than it is today. On the other hand shops were far less important to people than they are today. Can you think of any reasons why this was so?

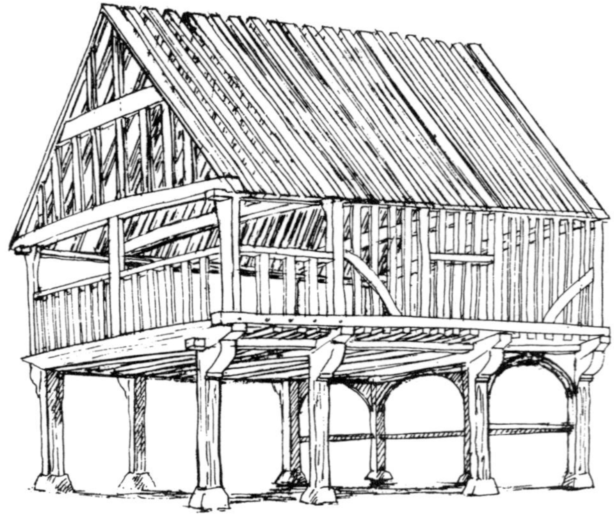

The timber-frame of Titchfield Market Hall

The upstairs part would usually have been used as a meeting room. Here the local council, or guilds of craftsmen, would meet to do business. We can see in this type of building, therefore, the ancestor of our town and county halls, which govern local community life today.

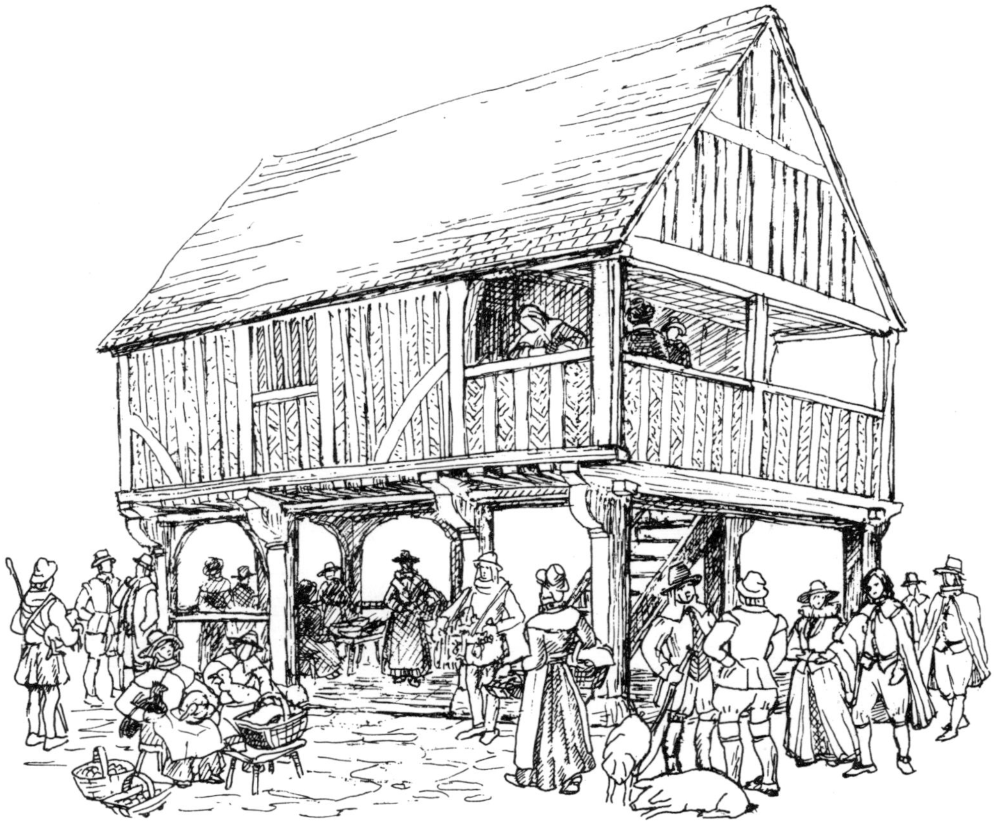

A market hall as it might have looked

THE HORSE GIN

The horse gin (or horse engine) came from Patching, near Arundel, and was once used for pumping water from a deep well. It was made about 1850 by Warner & Sons, engineers, of Cricklewood.

The machine is a one horse-power engine. The horse, walking round a circular stone path, was attached to the long wooden beam which turned a large cogwheel. This turned a smaller cogwheel which in turn drove three cranks connected to three pump rods. These rods go up and down inside the well to work the pump at the bottom.

The animal had to walk round and round at a steady pace of three miles per hour. Gins like this were often kept working for anything up to eight hours a day, and some country people who remember seeing them say how cruel the work seemed to be, and how they pitied the poor horse as it rotated the machinery hour after hour.

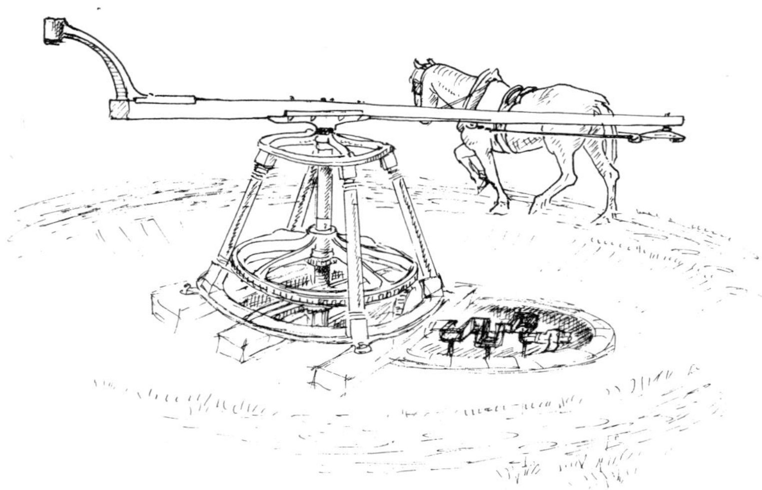

The gin makes an interesting comparison with the tread wheel at the Museum which was also used for raising water from a deep well. What do you think were the main differences between the two machines?

THE BLACKSMITH'S FORGE

Right on the edge of the Museum site is an old blacksmith's forge that used to be at Southwater, near Horsham. It is about a hundred years old.

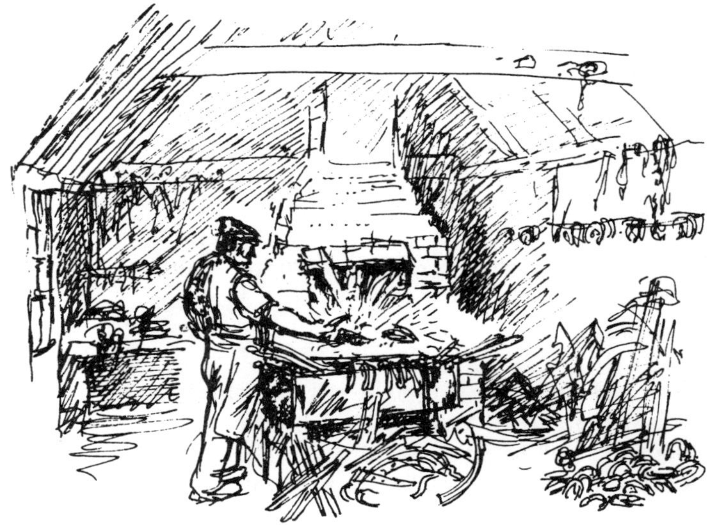

The blacksmith was once a very important part of every village, and his workshop always a place of great interest. From inside would come the steady beat of the bellows forcing air into the roaring fire, then the hammer ringing on the anvil as the softened iron was beaten and shaped into all sorts of useful things for the village people — horse shoes, equipment for the farmer, household articles for the cottager. In fact he made so many things that there was a time when no village could have possibly done without its blacksmith.

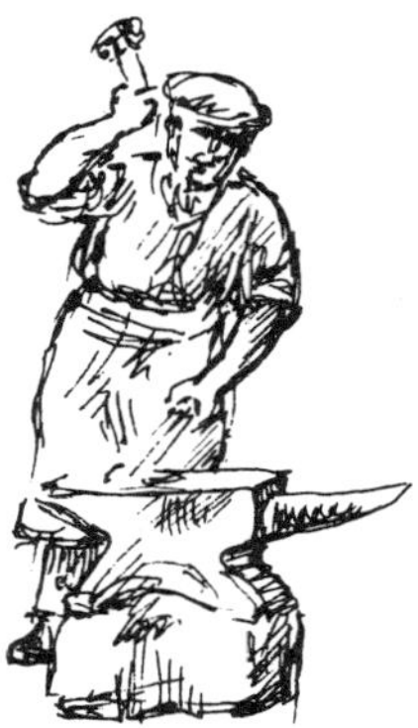

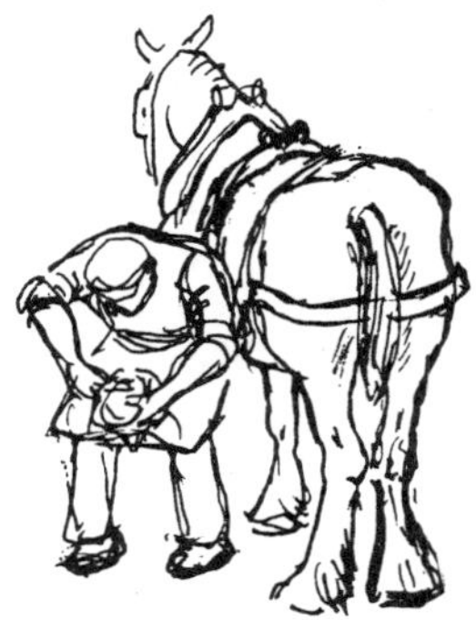

Have a look inside the forge and see how many blacksmith's tools you can see lying around. Notice also how the walls are made. They are built of upright split timbers, with the bark facing the outside.

THE WATERMILL AND WINDPUMP

In this corner of the Museum a start has been made to re-erect a watermill from Lurgashall, near Petworth. The mill is being rebuilt between two specially constructed mill ponds, an upper and a lower, to give a drop of at least twelve feet to turn the water-wheel. When finished the mill will be fully working.

By the side of the upper pond is a small windpump from Westham near Pevensey. Windpumps like this were once used for draining wet, marshy land. This one was made during the 19th century. The sails (or sweeps as they were often called in Sussex) are covered with canvas sailcloth to catch the wind. The cloth can be rolled up when the pump is not in use or when all the force of a very strong wind is not needed. The wooden disc makes sure that the sweeps stay in the wind when the wind changes direction. Underneath, between the supporting posts, you can see the pumping mechanism.

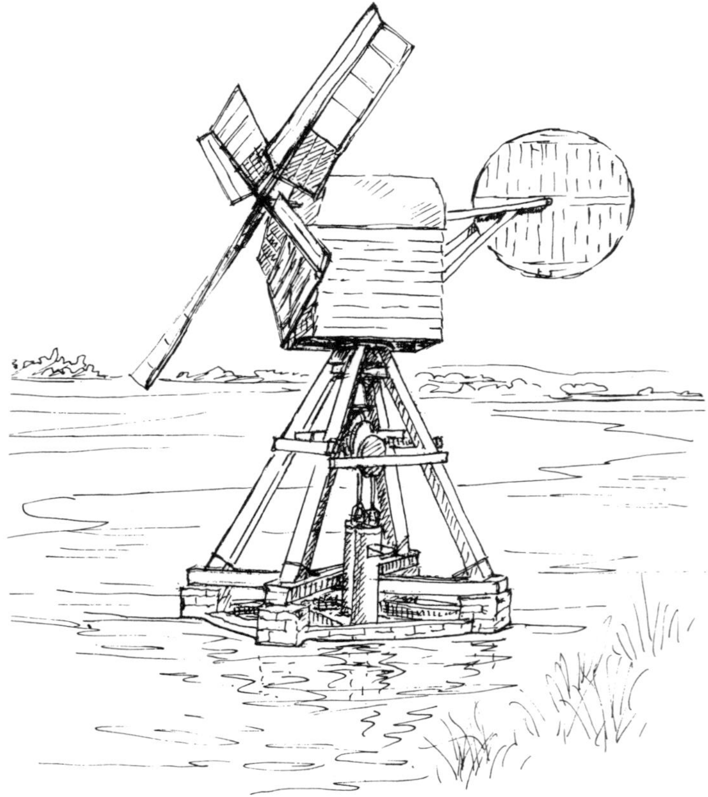

THE TOLL HOUSE

This tiny building came from Upper Beeding near Shoreham-by-Sea, and is called a toll house. It was built about 1807.

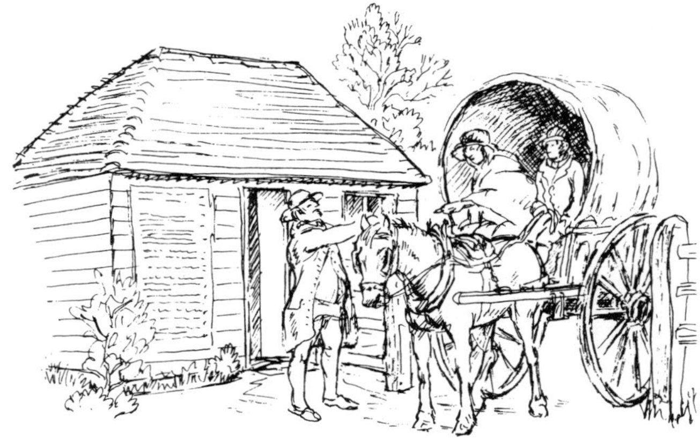

A hundred years ago there were many little houses like this all over the country, each one with a big gate outside which went across the road.

The reason for putting a gate across the road was that vehicles and animals had to be paid for before being allowed through the gate. This money that had to be paid was called a toll, and was used to keep the roads in repair.

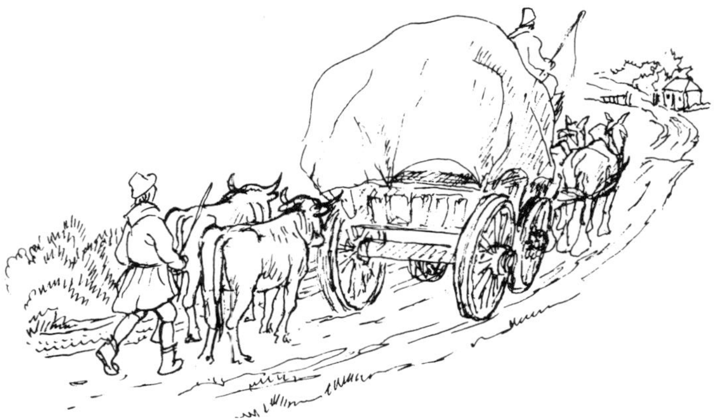

If people wished to use the roads there were lots of different charges. Have a look at the toll board fixed to the outside of the toll house and see the list of prices, and then try and find the answers to these questions:

1. Who could travel the cheapest on the road?

2. How much did it cost to take a score of sheep through the gate? (A 'score' means 20.)

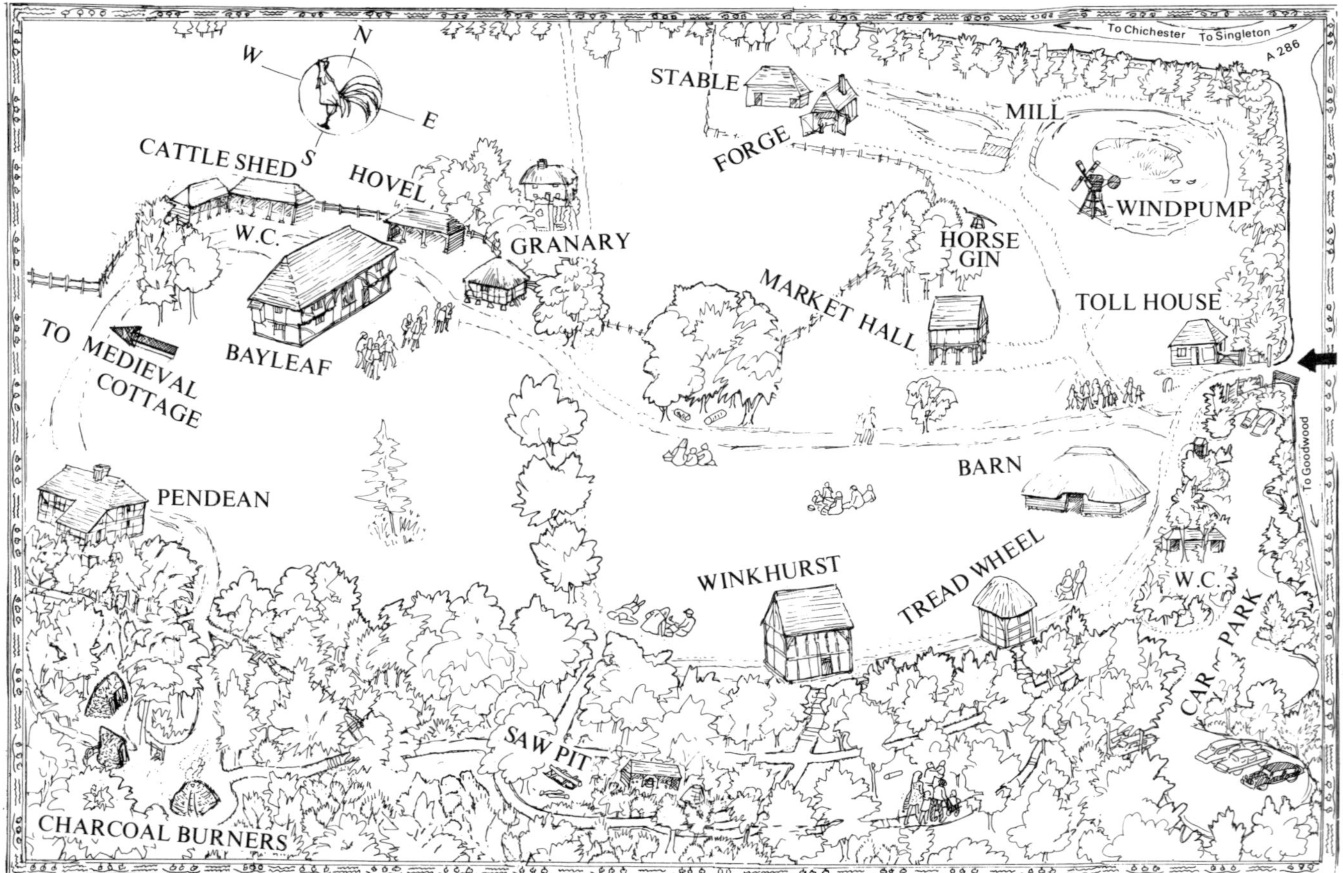

To Chichester
To Singleton
A 286
N
W
E
S
STABLE
FORGE
MILL
CATTLE SHED
HOVEL
W.C.
GRANARY
WINDPUMP
HORSE GIN
MARKET HALL
TOLL HOUSE
TO MEDIEVAL COTTAGE
BAYLEAF
To Goodwood
BARN
PENDEAN
WINKHURST
TREAD WHEEL
W.C.
CAR PARK
SAW PIT
CHARCOAL BURNERS

THINGS TO DO

Construction

Choose the building you liked seeing the best at the Museum, and make a model.

If you like making camps, construct a full-size copy of the charcoal burner's huts. These are very simple and need materials which are easy to collect together.

Reading

Read *Swallows and Amazons* and *Pigeon Post* by Arthur Ransome. These are adventure stories and include descriptions of charcoal burning.

Visit your local library and find books which will tell you about the way medieval people lived and worked. Find out about clothes, food, drink and furniture. You will then be able to understand something of the home life of Winkhurst and Bayleaf. There are also many story books on medieval times, such as *Ring Out Bow Bells* by Cynthia Harnett, and *Redcap Runs Away* by Rhoda Power.

Searching

Around your home or school find out if there are any

Toll houses and milestones.
Timber frame buildings (like Winkhurst and Bayleaf).
Old crafts still being worked. Are there any blacksmiths?
Donkey wheels and horse gins.

You could take photographs or make drawings of these, and then start a scrapbook.

Collecting

In your scrapbook collect information from newspapers and magazines about old buildings.

FOR YOUR OWN NOTES: